TRYSTS

LILA DUNLAP

Lunar Chandelier Collective

Lunar Chandelier Collective
(a subset of Lunar Chandelier Press)

lunarchandeliercollective.wordpress.com
lunarchandeliercollective@gmail.com

First edition.

ISBN 978-0-9986636-4-7

Cover design by Larry Chernicoff /
WindhorseCreative.com
Cover photo by Carmine De Fazio /
Unsplash.com

TRYSTS

CONTENTS

"Nothing Is Ever Right"

Nothing is ever right.
Rejoice in this fact.
I come, plump and red-
faced and stubbly legged.
My hair is dirty and my eyes
shine in the chilly morning.

How is love for the squirrels and bears?
Elk make Valentines Day cards
for one another. Bobcats
red-teethed run away
from the camera.

Learn our lessons from them
he whispered to me
under the bed.
He was my cousin and I
felt comfortable around him
without my corset.

As I never will be with you,
who are not my blood.
I am in love with the land
you till and are in, and the grass
which in fact is your back,
your hands and your tan
skin baling hay in the sun.

Nothing is ever wrong.
We roll around in the strawberry patch
and under the hops, their fragrant songs
igniting our faces with excitable oils
and promising us meetings
with the stars.

And when the day wanes,
and we get off work, we feel
the violin concertos of the birds
rapping in the trees, their downy faces
blood-red in the heat of the leaves,
life sap within them and on them.

Find order within what you do
without *you*, he said. Who I am
when I'm not being myself.

So at night when I lie
in the river-stream I call my bed
I can feel the pulse of the Earth
sending backwards and forwards
currents of love between mountain and ocean,
messages that will never be read.

AUBADE

the mist clears
night fades to day
it is hard to imagine
that that which is faded *to*
can fade— and yet here we are
grey haired and wet
between the legs
green-eyed and -eared
the scent of love hot on our necks
embarrassed and brave
watching the cars
begin to move in the morning
what for us is just
one long day
but koi in the fountain
are a little bigger,
we are a little younger
my lips are pink and swollen, I see,
when I look in the mirror,
as silver as God on days
after I've stayed up late,
and you are not real,
are not tired like myself
not constipated, not sticky
and nervous; you vanish
as soon as I leave
so that I can begin
thinking about you.

The way is left
said the right.
Your hand is

where I remember.
In our boat to
where we desired,

it was resting on the
steering mechanism.
I was relaxing

and reading
a newspaper
or a map, or

a poem out loud
I hope
it meant something

to you; you
were in charge
of the motion,

your swift strokes
or steers, depending
on what kind of

boat we were in,
pirogue, trireme, or
some white-sailed beauty,

genius of boatwright
meant for these cruises
sleepy and slow.

You know
true romance is never
passionate,

is more like what
we think "nature" is,
cool and damp

mutable, muggy,
reeds
and rats.

And the chambermaids throw
their dresses upon
the cool grass.

He says
I know,
I have seen

this pattern before.
You're exactly
who I thought

you were.
Tumble
down the wooden stairs

not for lack
of stars.
Show me

what you were
looking for
tonight.

I will meet you
under the
cake in the cupboard,

under the pads that
float on the pond
and the shapes that

darkly hover
near there
and the lights that

you've never really seen
except in your
desire.

Dream of
me for
I am

gone, as bright as
eggs cooked right
in their chickens

in the sun,
virginal in their
pecking

these
vernal ladies
got a fish

in her bucket
of well-
water this morning.

The name
of the god
changed

when you found out
who I was, luckily
you never will.

There are few
stepladders left
to the sky.

Meet me
where I was
when you met me

for the first time,
your last
chance for discovery.

I meant it
when I said
I was looking

over your shoulder,
you forgotten
sea-green statue

next to me,
us three
deceptive

Pan and
female Pan
do you hear

the blue-green grapes
and leaves
as white as

the sky
which we fade to
September

bound for the other
side, eyes tracking
back over

home-wood
work and
wonder

right where the wind
is afraid
to go in.

Excuse me, I seem
to have lost
my mouth

sprawled and bursting
flowers down where
no light ever sees

home to aqua
women of
ambiguous race.

You know the world
is coming apart,
dividing in two

he said
one half
magma

and the other
a frozen
ocean.

So were the thoughts
of the frogs
and their creepy spawn,

entrails
where I wanted
to swim.

Their green
goo the furthest
substance from sky.

So I had
to stay
in the clouds.

And here I am,
typing as if
I never learned

how to sin.
Of course you don't
believe me,

that I'm where
I've been
all along

where I landed
at the beginning
of the world

or sprung
from the ground
like an Athenian.

But we all are,
the king is
all of our fathers

and we
have many
of those.

Meet me in
the lowest stratum
of soil

that remembers no kings
only fights
between animals

where we are safe
in the realm
of all possible meanings

every combination
of words
and what

we might possibly
be trying
to say.

Don't think about
what you find yourself
thinking about.

Let it
think about
you.

Choose you
like you
chose me

because I could see
the weasels
in the snow

slinking
thru black
winter nights.

I can tell you
with my hands
how they moved.

In one ear
like a thought thru
the ether, *Aithēr*, corn

red and golden
chattering above
all the other vegetables.

In one.
And out the other.
Wind thru

telephones.
You can hear
them coming

whoever
they may
be

trains or
trams or
storms

clattering
thru the winter wind
and woods,

weeds all dead
in fields
rattling

words
without
words,

light
from
light.

Go into it.
Imperative
verbs

are the only
ones you'll need.
Mira

the child says
to her mother
in the grocery store

or at the park
on the swing or
in the pool.

Look what
I can
do.

Open fruits
with no hands.
Swim

around the world
just so I can
sneak up behind you.

Look, she says,
in her mother's second language,
Here is something

for me,
something
I need.

I draw to me
what will augment me
naturally.

I think
of nothing
else.

The world
is what happens
in the meantime.

The moon
rises, and the moon-plants
open their eyes.

Men and dreams,
voices and soft
hair.

Let us grow
by the second light
four hundred thousand

times less bright
in appearance than
the first, not forgetting

the hundreds of other
littler moons,
foxfires, noctiluca, ignis fatuus

that all derive
their freedom
from the sun,

for freedom
is light
and the ability

to enter
into it.
Draw me

a circle
of sky
just over

my shoulder
for looking into
any time.

The sun
is going down,
the girls

are drunk
in the millpond;
the young gentleman

having recently
discovered
his sexuality

resolves
to mate
with all of them.

The maids of his
estate, having finished
their work

for the day,
and having no
impending courtships

to grieve them
are excited
at the prospect.

The grass
and the air
are littered

with white feathers
drifting in the dim,
floating in the pool

stuck to frilly
or practical undergarments,
loose

amidst the onset
of night
as if

pieces of the sun
itself, clinging to
the day that preceded

and now is dying
somewhere
in the hills.

It seems
to the girls
as if

a blue mist
is rolling in
and shrouding their scene

now
are their selves
whole planets

to which
the mist sticks
but does not surrender.

Neither
does it remember
nor obliterate

the deeds
of the past
which find their homes

in human minds
and in the soil.
The gentleman

performs supremely
for his young age
and seems to participate

for a time
in the perpetual waves
of changing pleasures

enjoyed
by the maids
both young and old.

Back at home,
at the place
where no one lives

a light
comes on
in the attic.

Just as, in fact,
it always has,
but we never noticed

because
we were
living there.

TAROT

from Ashley Garrett's series
of paintings, "Tarot"

Image 1

Hungry girls need to eat
even if it means this cactus.
Yum, prickly floral, rouge and rogue
maroon sideburns on starkly
stern gentleman of the desert
red rust bust underneath
his low shoulder, carrying little
but his beans and clean air.

Image 2

Big fist make little difference,
said the fish to the ruined
submarine. Kiss my kelp,
touch my mine, where the rusted spines
of this vintage bomb
talk to the tickling barnacles
when you dive down to find sharks
or treasure. The ghosts of dead sailors
dance drunk with anemones
reddish-coloured rainbows
just out of light of the shallows.

Image 3

The road blows bran
misted memory of vineyards
at the close of October
I can't help but think of Van Gogh's
twisted *Wheatfield with Crows,*
or so I remember,
the last dance before death
(for both the artist and the land)
a girl in a brown dress
empties grain onto the earth
its own winter soup
thick and meaty
rich with oil and complete starches
as rainbow and ruinous
as vaginal fluid
dripping after a rainstorm.

Image 4

Big blue blustery solid
genital rush.
This is a solid expulsion
via which we view the organ.
She shows us how deep
we need to go
to reach her manhood.
She keeps a little bit of sand
in the corner of her room.
And a leggy red bird
spreads its wings
right at the fulcrum
where she opens her legs.
Meanwhile Amazonian black ants
trickle out from inside her
willingly.

Image 5

Our bubbling fades to reverence
and we gratefully stand at attention
ready to kill or give birth to our god,
see him wash up unspoken of
on the sand. Ask me
was the water blue or grey
that day, was the sand of coral or glass?
Face-down we worship you,
strenuous as our worship is,
make us a cult for you,
and we rub down our temple with blood,
our window frames with lead paint,
and look to the larger sea that awaits us,
across that thin and whistling bridge.

Image 6

Begins with rose, ends with a leap,
End me, cries the Heavens,
see me splatter. He adds his hands
to the apple, and we find ourselves
soaring fast through the firmament.
Nothing happens but creation.
Watch the world work,
being everything inside its orgasm.

Image 7

A blue swivel, an Inuit child
asleep in his blankets of fur.
Outside the night rages on,
as unannounced and wild as any city.
Flocks of lantern-bearing or lantern-
        headed ghosts
prance by, outside on the snow.
Nearby, an eel sleeps, pulsing, his belly
full of food, and beyond this mess
of broadness and particularity
the sky makes its way to a hazy morning.

Image 8

A Christmas of who or what
has never seen the light
(as all Christmases are).
The wolf on spider legs salutes the rising red
and howls as best he can. Some snot
escapes through his teeth,
and he can see that it is green.
Upward white Christmas trees dash and dance:
Spruce and Fir we are! Yule-logs
to be set on fire by our Lord.
And God like a flaming Ferris-wheel
having buried one son bears another
and the demon turns his dark cloak
to cover his dirty blue face.

Image 9

The holiday cake is round.
The celebratory bread.
Babka, king cake, gallette du rois,
a holy circle,
(all but the Yule log, not Christian at all).
And here you can see
the brandied cherries
studding the sun,
shielding our eyes from our God
while the fuzzy blue sky
with the help of this warmth
ripples like silk in springtime ecstasy.

So round and round the ladies dance,
the girls of our village,
feet in the dirty grass
immune to filth, elevating the cake,
the coin, the loop,
the face that looks back at the heavens
and recognizes it as such.

Image 10

Under the water the wretched fish of the deep
cannot aptly celebrate the birth of our Lord,
but they do their best.
They swim fast in a circle
and maintain between them
a sprig of Christmas vegetation
dotted with berries and tied with ribbons
to complete their undersea wreath.
I don't know what to think of this tradition.
It is said that when our Christ was born,
at that same moment the cat Christ,
and dog Christ, and giraffe Christ,
and crab Christ were also born,
each according to his species.
That being said, my grandma also told me
that: "A fish isn't an animal,"
so it is hard to pass judgment on this one.

Image 11

Little dance moths
do during the day
-light hours, a book of hours
is the very progression of the sun
as we see it from our gardens.
The text is the squashes
fattened on the vine.
Healthy cucurbits
mumbling psalms
in late afternoon.
A blue bird lands
on the sprout of a pumpkin
suddenly weightless
in this quiet wind
of paradise, a walled garden, aware
and looking at itself and all else
surrounded by night
beyond the wall
and the dusky rhythms
of the jittering blood
within the dancers
exchanging their skin
with one another and the cosmos
make this brightness possible.

QUATRAINS IN THE OLD YEAR

1. The Miracle

The sea closed in on my trembling body,
and I was surrounded by infinite possibility.
A pea-green cloud enshrouded my jungle,
birds were cackling. I was cold as I was afraid.

Pendrill was looking at me, as I was for him.
I wished for a cave and a rainstorm.
Smothering gases rising, I peeped round the
   banister
and saw his waistcoat buttons glittering,
   blue and gold.

I found him chatting with the man serving
   hors d'oeuvres.
My horse was waiting. Later, as we were watching
   some ninny play the piano,
I stared straight ahead and didn't do anything.
He was waiting in the barn.

He had a silver cask full of water
and waited out the storm in the hay.
He refilled his bottle with a trickle from the roof
and enjoyed the smell of the animals.

He urinated into the hay. The smoke cleared.
I was ready to stay awake for three days
and take a bath in the freezing stream.
It was Christmas.

I choked him with holly
and wept when he passed out.
The tears streamed out from my arms,
and I held his cock until the sun rose.

2. Falles

My hair is greasy in the woods.
I'm saying everything I've always been saying
but that you've never heard.
Children lifted to the gods.

On sticks. Beams. Fathers weep
as the sun turns red.
The fire-goddess snakes down the mountain
in the form of hundreds of men.

The coats of shaggy bears turn to gold.
I'm just along for the ride.
Hope nobody minds.
And they don't.

3. Sensorium

Resigned I lie in the hay which is emerald.
Sapphire rose of an eye
looking down thru the slats, peering
       thoughtfully.
Dragonflies puncture the ceiling.

Incense of frankincense or jasmine
rolls out from the rocks.
An altar, not a tomb,
beckons the insects to worship.

Animals with silver moustaches
clamber about my shelter, they are
ringing their bells, smoking cigars
as thick as Pendrill's member.

I rinse myself in the tub
and give them the water to drink.
My breasts are as big as volcanoes,
my legs as wide as this river-valley.

4. Origin

I have already written this poem.
Blue-lagoon perfume. You swan,
wash your hair in my cucumber lather,
cool and smooth on your pearls.

My silky hands sedate you.
I am your grandmother.
I run my tongue around your navel
while you descend the staircase of sleep.

Casks of pea-green wood being moved to Babylon
by boat, I croon, my touch
is as mossy as oak or elk
antlers. The siren lighthouse comes around

honing your heart to its rounds.
Leave me by candlelight, waking
as the mistress demands you, humming.
Remember how I touched you.

5. The Key to It All

Into the dark and gloom living room
burns tulsi basil, scent of her holiness
Saint Cecelia, Cecily, Sicily, bless me
with warm hands and neck.

The oil lamps burn, the frankincense,
stuccoed walls, drywall,
over which the key to it all is plastered
chipping Victorian lime.

I slam on these walls with a hammer,
break the plaster away, collect
the pieces in my oaken basket
and grind them with water into mush

to re-seal these walls
of horseshit and my own hair
to make them pleasant on the inside
while I'm reading or taking a bath.

Colors fill them. The light
of my language is stained glass in the dark
Victorian parlor, for that's where we live,
who we are, and deny it.

The room moves to my music,
I wrote these poems while out in the hay
earlier, dreaming of my dream-lover

while the sun was high in the sky.

No harm in that. The hay was dry, and
I had something to talk about.
Now, in the dark wet of house-light,
something talks about me.

And I have little choice but to listen,
as warm as the blood in your heart.

PASTORAL DREAM AT SUPPERTIME

The smell of food being cooked
is near me. I am a lord, but
I am not lord over my senses.
I smell the rich fish and chicken,
lentils stewing in wine,
chickpeas and flower of squash, fried,
nut-breads and salads, delicious
marzipan, eggs, and cheese
in sauce of parsley and cream.

A piano plays next to my head.
I am living in the future.
I am asleep
next to the window.
Outside, I imagine
I can hear the sheep munching
great flocks of spinach,
heads of lettuce, the sounds
from their mouths are the meat of great
speeches.

And the fruits rot on the vine.

Craunch craunch go the teeth,
decimating crumply sheaths
attacking clean leaves, making it
mush for a holy stomach
smush under grinding flat teeth

pulverize grass and greens, loving
bellies provide the necessary fluids
for grazing herbivores, tramps
stomping the dewy valleys
with their gnashing plant-crunching jaws
grinding fresh leaves into mush.

Glowing flat ears of the grass
neat patches of moss
tramped on by steeds
carefully mashed into dust.

DREAM

Low dangling breasts
teat of the grass
spring cheeses, rich cows
chewing and making milk
inside them
two human breasts
over there in the field
I can see them, tho the sun
is blocking my face
they are so pale they are almost blue
yet they are flushed
like they've been running
uphill, are they here to meet me?
are they my mother's breasts?
are they my friends?
no, these breasts are mine,
grassy-smelling, Aphrodite's
blue boobs.   Yellow lemon blooms
small as silk in clusters
peek up thru the dewy grass
deep as emeralds, breezy
and chilly, the back of my neck
ripples, it must be morning
I can hear the cows
or sheep chewing, lowing,
this is good grass for cheese
I think, tasty and fresh
makes happy ewes
the breasts are radiant, smile at me,

but if I touch them they will be cold
I think, I'm not sure
how I can be looking at them
if they're mine, if I'm over here…
The thought consumes me.

ROSE

This courtyard
is where we lay our heads.
This chalice
is the water from our hands.
I know where to go because
I have nowhere to go.
Know me. Be my nose.
Take me smelling
along these summer streets
aperitifs of rose water, spaghetti,
incense, and watch
my feet turn into dust, my shoes
lost by the onset of dusk.

MOON BELLY

I pull my shirt up
to show you my belly
a moon like these two here
the faces of people I love
the faces of lions carved from stone
guarding the peristyle,
staring into the bayou,
serene and smooth
like ducks asleep in trees
like the stone bridges
brushing palmettoes.
I am only my belly,
as clear and blue and empty and black
as night in City Park in the Spring,
the ancient playground in the moonlight.

CHRISTMAS MYSTERY
OF THE MILLION ANIMALS

(I feel a million animals
multiplying in the sky
and in the dirt)
their chests like shields
or yellow roses
boasting big breasts
forcing their ways thru the woods
forest of scattered lights
that come from the beasts
themselves, their limbs glow
at midnight, off and on
glowworms but huge
quadrupeds, sheep and mares,
stoats lighting up
in and out of their holes
the animals are alive, alive
tonight, tonight

NAUTA, NAUTAE

Nauta, sailor, *poeta*, poet,
what a coincidence,
the two noblest professions
a man can endeavor to do
award him an honorary alpha
deign him an honorary girl

a true alpha male
is feminine,
agricola, farmer, that one too,
to know the dark earth
and its magic sap,
the mysterious mumblings,
the bottom of the body
from which language springs

brave, black knowledge
of places howling with winds
and earthquakes
where gods live
and satisfy themselves
it is treacherous even
to say this much
to pose to answer
such taboo questions as
Where do seeds come from?
Where do winds go to sleep?
What lies over that hill?

That one, by the crooked tree
and the sunbeam
questions men
don't like to think about
weak as they naturally are
but not all of them
some of them are brave enough
to act like girls,
to seek out knowledge of the sea.

ALFRED

Hair black as belts
the door bolted shut
in his linen nightgown, he
resists the urge to throw himself in the sea.

Or is that me?
I will lie down beside him
and get him to tell me a story.
He is bold tho his cheeks are pink.

The hair of a king.
Long and oily
and fragrant
as if he takes many and frequent
herbal baths.

I will wait for him to touch me
leery with the night,
heavy eyelids and shoulderblades,
birds with curtains for wings.

He does kind of look like a girl.
O the cool summer nights
of Wessex, breathing
like a field of sleeping horses,
stones at peace, and we breathing
into each other's hair and dreams
and the velvet canopy.

DOROTHY

My face gleams like a balloon, a balloon
that one day I will leave in
unnoticed, on the soft side of town
I'll take off, on a bright blue day
that isn't in any month
a day that just *is*
maybe a Tuesday
and the countryside will be as it was
before factories and pavement
before poverty and smoke
sparkling, tinkling
bells on cows,
little bridges over glistening streams
the kind Raggedy Ann and Andy
might fall into
if they're not careful
I will float
as light as linen
nobody with me, nobody even
thinking of me
maybe even no God
staring down
just the blue and the green
and the white clouds bright
maybe without even a sun
just bright all by themselves
I can hear the wind whistling
around the ropes tied to the basket
I'm in, kissing them

I can sit down if I like
in my t-shirt and jeans
and know that nobody is thinking about me
that I don't need anything
that I will be here forever
until the end of time
and then I won't.

CAITLIN

And yet I am not even here,
here I am
on the beach of your infrastructure
booing, yawning, mooing
changing my dress
chewing my sandwich on the sand
as the mist rises up, blown from the sea
the mermaids help with their lips
to lift it
into fishermen's ships
leisurely lounging in your eye
or not, what do I care
what time of day or week it is
bubbling, rolling
into and out of the surf
in my see-thru white dress
unsexed, but I guess
you can un-do me
if you like
or not
what do I care
the fog is as thick as me
my thick hair thick
as smoke in the game-rooms
boy I sure do love this meat and cheese
my toes in the sand
it is after midnight
in Mississippi
it is three pm

in Wales
what do I care
where I sing my song
the windows are all my windows
every town provides me my windows
I am leisure, I am lift
I am rolling in
and out of the surf
the clams and crabs know
I have always been here
I will always be here
as long as the tide comes in
and rolls out, covering the banks,
leaving puddles and rockpools
along the holy shore.

THE MOON IS BLUE

Under it all
asleep like a blanket
pulled up to her chin
a child
with huge cheeks
rubbing her eyes.

The stars are cardboard
or paper cut-outs.
Matisse's last work
was gouaching the sky
the mystery of night
and the afterlife
feel him here
above the trees
working, see,
you can see from your balcony.

The pears are of
phenomenal size
as big as the cheeks of the child.
Suggesting that it might
be night, that you live
in a climate that's received you.

January opens the breeze.
Balcony beckons you
out onto the sky.
It's warm or not.

The pears have hardened themselves
in your heart, or not.
You wish on the leaves
you see moving before you.
You will make perry out of these pears
or chutney.
You will move yourself
to their sways.
They are plump and luscious
and bursting at the skin
in January.

The moon is blank
with black stars.
You give yourself to the breeze.
There is more to be
than there are rivers in
this river-valley.

--

The ice springs forth
from the mountains
crusting the cliffs,
closing the roads,
but it is warm down in the river-valley.
A loose breeze blows
thru the strange wooden town
like peeling oranges
on a table.

Lanterns float
above doors.
Boats meander
on various waters
blowing and slowly
leaving lovely hills
to see themselves to shore.

Who lives here? you dream.
Me, you tell yourself, realizing
that there can be no other answer,
me.

THE OLIVE-MERCHANT'S MISTRESS

I can't seem to find anyone
to listen. Now here you are.
Show me how to harvest olives, again,
how to lay out nets under the trees
and wait for them to fall.

My dress is thin and colorful,
and she sees me when I'm coming.
You will wait for me, won't you?
under your terracotta roof
that the rain beats on as big as olives
once a year, when I come trudging back
from my spot in the sun, having waited for you
under my chiffon and muslin
now covered with the mud of your driveway
sticking to my legs like river-sludge
stuck to the fur of two rats in the gutter
making love.

THE BLUE FAIRY

Drooping down a night breeze
to talk to me
uninvited, red and glowing,
is a midnight phantom;
he says,
You know it's possible to control
the rate of the flow of ideas?
You can slow down, you know.
You can sit
by the side of the road
and pretend to eat a sandwich.

You don't have
to do any of this.

The blue fairy appears
and puts me to sleep
by the power of the living forest
and the wind of the wooden structures,
mostly abandoned,
around my house.

I sleep like a dove on a rock.
The red fish-phantom with his thick black
outline
does not bother me.

LIBERATION POEM

Huddled under
a serious yellow blanket
I look outside
and imagine what could be there
if I were who I ought to be
if I didn't bring *me* along
for the ride
every time.

The birdbath is smothered in snow.
The birdbath tries my nerves.
Fill me up, he commands,
Wreathe me in flowers.

Florita brings out the jug
and fills him up.
Her flowers are feet upon the new grass.
She is not a person.

The urn is sandy grey-red.
I fill it up at the faucet
and water my flowers.
This, I realize, is the person
            who gets in my way.
The flower-waterer.
Suddenly the sky fills with clouds
and the earth is showered in rain.

I am watered.
I am a living organism,
wretched and capable of dance.

I am not an irrigator.
I am not responsible for civilization.

MANCY

Clever
we could be
if we knew
how to take no for an answer.

The candle breaks in its glass.
Or did I break it?
Knocked it over
onto the floor
spilling wax, glass
at night, after we'd turned out the lights

The stars say no.
It's over. Done.
What you were trying
to rid yourself of
is gone. Now go to bed.
And look out the windows to see
what is really going on:
Snow flurries around the streetlamps at midnight,
on your street
and in your endless heart.